THE GROUCH

T0316259

Molière

THE GROUCH

A modern version of
Le Misanthrope by
RANJIT BOLT

OBERON BOOKS
LONDON

First published in 2008 by Oberon Books Ltd
521 Caledonian Road, London N7 9RH
Tel: 020 7607 3637 / Fax: 020 7607 3629
e-mail: info@oberonbooks.com
www.oberonbooks.com

Copyright © Ranjit Bolt 2008

Ranjit Bolt is hereby identified as author of this translation in
accordance with section 77 of the Copyright, Designs and Patents
Act 1988. The author has asserted his moral rights.

All rights whatsoever in this work are strictly reserved and
application for performance etc. should be made before
commencement of rehearsal to The Agency Ltd, 24 Pottery Lane,
London W11 4LZ. No performance may be given unless a licence
has been obtained, and no alterations may be made in the title or
the text of the play without the author's prior written consent.

This book is sold subject to the condition that it shall not by way
of trade or otherwise be circulated without the publisher's consent
in any form of binding or cover or circulated electronically other
than that in which it is published and without a similar condition
including this condition being imposed on any subsequent
purchaser.

A catalogue record for this book is available from the British
Library.

ISBN: 978-1-84002-835-5

www.bloomsbury.com

Characters

ALAN

PHILIP

ORVILLE

CELIA

BATES

CHRIS

LORD ARNE

EILEEN

FAY

*All the characters in this play, including their beliefs
and opinions, are fictional; any resemblance to people
alive or dead is entirely coincidental.*

The Grouch was first performed at West Yorkshire Playhouse on 15 February 2008, with the following cast:

ALAN, Allan Corduner

PHILIP, Steven Pinder

ORVILLE, Habib Nasib Nader

CELIA, Denise Gough

BATES, Andrew Price

CHRIS, Benedict Sandiford

LORD ARNE, Christopher Ettridge

EILEEN, Kate Miles

FAY, Lizzie Hopley

Director Sarah Esdaile

Designer Ruari Murchison

Lighting Designer Malcolm Rippeth

Composer Simon Slater

Sound Designer Mic Pool

Movement Joyce Henderson

Act One

CELIA's drawing room.

ALAN (sitting on a sofa), PHILIP, both with glasses of wine.
There is a bowl of nuts on a table to which PHILIP keeps helping
himself during the following.

PHILIP: Alan? (*Silence.*) What's wrong?

ALAN: Leave me alone!

PHILIP: You're the oddest man I've ever known!
               Our friendship *veers* from peak to trough.

ALAN: Look, will you kindly just piss off!

PHILIP: Not till you've let me have my say.

ALAN: Why should I, after that display? (*Points off.*)

PHILIP: Please, just be calm and hear me out.

ALAN: And what's there to be calm about?

PHILIP: But why take *umbrage* in this way?
               We're friends, but I'm the first to…

ALAN: Eh?
     Friends are we? *I'm* not friends with *you!*
     Not after that just now. (*Points off again.*) It's true
     That I have hitherto professed
     To be your friend, but I protest
     I cannot be so any more –
     Not when you're *rotten* to the core!

PHILIP: Me? Rotten? *How,* in Heaven's name?

ALAN: Dear God, you ought to die of shame!
     Such insincere behaviour must
     Fill decent people with disgust:
     You seemed so eager to embrace
     And praise that fellow, to his face,
     You *fluttered* with affection, now
     Making an offer or a vow,
     Now telling him the sweetest things

(As if your fervent fondlings
Were not enough for anyone)
Yet when I asked you, once he'd gone,
Who the man was, and whence he came
You scarcely even knew his name!
Your ardour vanished like a mist,
He might as well just not exist!
Why, it's unworthy, a disgrace,
Dishonest, cowardly and base!
Where's your integrity? If *I'd*...
Not that I could do if I tried...
But *if* I ever acted thus
I'd hang myself, no mess no fuss!

PHILIP: So one's to hang for not being rude?
What a peculiar attitude!
That is a sentence I'm inclined
To waive this time, if you don't mind –
(*Chuckling.*) I'm lenient with myself, I know...

ALAN: Droll, is it? *I* don't find it so.

PHILIP: Come, come, what would you have me do?

ALAN: Be *honourable, sincere* and *true,*
Speak always, *only,* from the heart.

PHILIP: So were a man to come and start
Ecstatically embracing you
You wouldn't feel it proper to
Pay him in like coin, seem as fond
Of him as he of you, respond
In kind to praise and promises
And, as he's scratched your back, scratch his?

ALAN: No! I deplore the bogus ways
Of society these days,
I loathe these facile fools who fall
Over themselves to kiss and maul
And crawl to everyone they meet,
Lace every greeting with 'my sweet'
And never say a word they mean,

8

It's not just stupid, it's obscene,
A sort of national contest
To find out who can arse-lick best;
What use is it to have a man
Telling me he's my biggest fan,
Praising me, promising to be
My friend for all eternity
If he has feelings just as strong
For the next bloke who comes along?
Who wants respect they have to share
With everybody everywhere?
That isn't what respect's *about* –
The word *implies* being *singled out.*
Since you've espoused the current trend
I can no longer be your friend,
Sorry, but I despise a heart
Of which the whole world owns a part,
That's just not good enough for me,
In friendship I demand to be
One man in ten, not one of nine,
The nation's chum cannot be mine.

PHILIP: We're in the world, for Heaven's sake,
There *are* concessions we must make
To simple social *politesse* –
Would you defy convention?

ALAN: Yes!
I'll hound these rogues without remorse,
I'll stop their bogus intercourse!

PHILIP: Their what?!

ALAN: This endless *bonhomie*
That's not what it purports to be,
This *trade* in counterfeit goodwill.
I'm going to make mankind fulfil
Its proper function.

PHILIP: Which is what?

ALAN: *To tell the truth!* Let's stop the rot,

> Let's all the time and everywhere,
> No matter who the hell is there,
> Proclaim exactly what we feel,
> No flattery, but just our real,
> Untempered view, straight down the line,
> Right from the entrails, every time!

Enter BATES. He picks up their (now empty) glasses and is taking them out.

PHILIP: Oh, Bates, please take these nuts away
Before I scoff the lot.

BATES collects the bowl of nuts, and goes out.

> Okay
> Where were we?

ALAN: Honesty.

PHILIP: Ah yes,
> Well, it's a virtue – nonetheless
> It can at times be out of place,
> Absurd, depending on the case;
> With due respect to your stern creed,
> All of us sometimes feel the need
> To hide our actual sentiments,
> I mean, it simply makes no sense
> To charge about just letting on
> To anyone and everyone
> Exactly what we think of them,
> It'd create complete mayhem.
> Someone you hate comes up to you
> And greets you – what are you to do?
> Say 'Fuck off, you obnoxious prat!'?

ALAN: Yes! *I* would say *exactly* that!

PHILIP: So take that old frump Emily –
You'd tell her that at sixty-three
She can't look thirty, and her face,
With its cosmetic carapace
And nips and tucks and botox sheen
Looks quite preposterous, nay, obscene?

ALAN: I would.

PHILIP: I see. And you'd tell Dan
          That he is the most boring man
          In London, with the anecdotes
          He's always ramming down our throats?

ALAN: Of course! Let's have one man round here
          Who, Heaven help us, is *sincere!*
          I tell you, I shall spare no one –
          I witness such *foul* goings-on
          It makes me physically sick –
          A *crust* of evil inches thick
          Is covering our society –
          I *choke* with bile at what I see –
          Injustice everywhere one looks –
          Flatterers, traitors, fraudsters, crooks.
          But worst of all, and by a mile –
          The foremost failing and most vile,
          Of these dark days, at least for me,
          Is the sheer bullshit of *PC:*
          We walk on eggshells all the time
          Scared to commit the heinous crime
          Of being blunt or frank (sincere
          In other words); we live in fear
          That what we say may give offence –
          Be taken in a hostile sense
          By someone, or some group, whose skin
          Is so ridiculously thin
          That if we merely said 'Hello!'
          Or 'Lovely weather!' off they'd go
          Demanding an apology!
          One touchy twerp can sometimes be
          Death to a man's entire career…
          Sorry, I've had it up to here
          With this insane, inane charade,
          You say I take it all too hard
          But one jot more and I'll explode!
          I'm telling you, the only road

Now open to me is to *flee!*
I'm finished with society.

PHILIP: Alan…

ALAN: It's either them or me.
I'm allergic to the human race.

PHILIP: (*Aside:*) The man's an absolute head-case!
(*Aloud, to ALAN:*) Since frankness is your great *forté*
Let *me* be frank with *you* and say:
This curious disease you've caught
Of always speaking your first thought,
The way that everywhere you go
You rant and rave, and puff and blow,
And put the whole world in the dock
Has rendered you a laughing-stock.

ALAN: I wouldn't have it otherwise!
I'm laughed at, am I? Well, one tries!
I thank you for that heartening news –
I can't think what I'd rather lose
Than my contemporaries' respect –
They're all such fools that, in effect,
Appearing wise to them would be
A sign of imbecility!

PHILIP: Do you *despise* your fellow men?

ALAN: Are eggs the product of a hen?

PHILIP: All of them? You leave no one out?
A general loathing? What about…
I don't know…surely *every* age
Boasts the odd saint and the odd sage?

ALAN: Not this one! Hence my wholesale hate –
There's *no one* I don't execrate.
People are either evil, or
Simply by failing to abhor
The evil ones' behaviour, they
Condone it, in a tacit way.
Look at this lawsuit I've got now:
How can society allow

12

The swine I'm fighting to *exist*
Still less, implicitly assist
His machinations? His veneer
Fools no one – it is crystal clear
To everyone who knows the man
That he's a fraud, a charlatan,
A lying, scheming hypocrite,
A total, twenty-carat shit;
And yet he's welcome everywhere,
With his smug, sanctimonious air,
And if the bastard wants something
That needs a bit of networking,
Some contract, post, or God-knows-what,
He'll snap it up, he'll scheme and plot
And beat far better men than him.
Despite being talentless and dim.
But that's the way the system works,
These grasping, money-grubbing *jerks*
Are given quarter, nay, much more –
That's why I often hanker for
A different life, in some bleak spot
Untainted by mankind.

PHILIP: What rot!
Your moral doctrine's much too stern,
You seem to want us to return
To Cato's Rome! It can't be done,
Those heady days are dead and gone,
You ask too much of modern man,
You'll never change him – *no one* can.
I witness people doing wrong,
I see their evil, smell its pong,
But I keep quiet and hold my nose,
I don't start firing off salvos
Of indignation!

ALAN: If *you* met
With treachery (which you haven't yet) –
A friend betrayed you, or your wealth

13

Was filched from you by guile and stealth,
Or noxious calumnies were spread
About you, then, for all you've said,
Do you suppose you'd simply sit
Impassively and swallow it
With total, philosophic calm?

PHILIP: I shouldn't feel the least alarm;
It's part and parcel of our lot –
We're human beings, are we not,
By definition, gravely flawed.
I won't, I never have, deplored
Such actions. No, they trouble me
No more than if I were to see
A vulture pick a carcass, say,
Or monkeys snatch my lunch away,
Or wolves…

ALAN: All right, I get your drift.
So I'm not even to be *miffed*
When I've been wronged, nay, torn to shreds,
Let's all sit tight and keep our heads
Whatever we're subjected to!

PHILIP: Exactly.

ALAN: Well, that just won't do.

PHILIP: You would do well to hold your peace,
Stop fulminating without cease
Against this enemy of yours
And *work* to further your own cause,
Take *steps,* I mean, to win your suit.

ALAN: I shan't devote one minute to it.
Whatever made you think I might?

PHILIP: Alan, you *must* put up a fight
And *I* can't help you, I'm afraid.

ALAN: I wasn't going to seek your aid.
Justice, at least, is on my side.

PHILIP: Oh, dear! I don't suppose you've tried
        Pulling a few strings anywhere?

ALAN: There'll be no need for that, will there?
        I'm in the right.

PHILIP: Oh, use your head!
        Wasn't it you who just now said
        How bad the world is? How good men
        Get shat on time and time again?

ALAN: True.

PHILIP: There you are then! *He'll* pull strings,
        Use contacts, try all sorts of things –
        You're going to have to do the same
        And beat him at his own vile game.
        There's every chance you'll win the day.

ALAN: Pull strings? I can't. That's not my way.
        I'll go down nobly with the ship!
        I'll throw the thing!

PHILIP: Oh, get a grip!
        Your enemy has powerful friends,
        In order to attain his ends
        He'll stop at nothing…

ALAN: Excellent!
        He'll win, then, and I'll be content!

PHILIP: Content?

ALAN: I'll make it a test case
        To show how low the human race
        Has sunk, how wicked it's become
        That it can let such wrongs be done
        In public, to a man like me!

PHILIP: (*Aside:*) Oh, what's the use? He's off his tree!

ALAN: I'm telling you, I *want* to lose,
        I don't care what the hell ensues,
        To prove a point I'll blow my suit.

PHILIP: (*Shaking his head and smiling wryly.*)
        My goodness, but you *are* a hoot!

ALAN: You find it funny? More fool you.

PHILIP: This…*rectitude* you're so into,
This *probity* that you demand
From everybody, out of hand,
D'you find it in the girl you love?
I'm puzzled – you're so leery of
Humanity in general, yet
It's *her* on whom your sights are set,
Her of all people; why so keen
On *her,* when women like Eileen,
Whose goodness is as plain as day,
And clever, sober, serious Fay
Are obviously sold on you?
Their charms you seem impervious to,
But Celia, who's malicious, vain,
A…let's not use a nasty name –
Who likes her men, at any rate –
In short, who stands for all you hate
About society these days,
Embodies its degenerate ways,
Can twist you round her…

ALAN: Yes. I know.
I see her failings, even though
I'm mad on her, and what I see
I censure, unreservedly,
She's *chock-a-block* with wickedness
But I adore her nonetheless;
I both acknowledge and condemn
Her faults, and there's a host of them,
But when we meet I go weak-kneed
And quite forget my moral creed,
Her loveliness is just too great.
But through my love I'll inculcate
A different mindset into her –
I'll fumigate her, as it were,
Of any taint of this vile time.

PHILIP: You've picked an Everest to climb.
            D'you reckon *she* loves *you*?

ALAN: Oh, yes –
            I wouldn't love a girl unless
            It was requited.

PHILIP: If it's clear
            She loves you, why do you still fear
            And deprecate your rivals?

ALAN: Why?
            I'm mad about the girl, aren't I?
            I want her all, not just a share,
            In fact, I've come here to declare
            Precisely that to Celia now.

PHILIP: I've not had time for love somehow
            But if I had I tell you who
            I'd pay my own attentions to
            And that's her cousin – yes, Eileen,
            I mean to say, you must have seen
            She's mad about you, how on earth
            Can you ignore her obvious worth?
            She's charming, unpretentious – she...
            Is so much more your cup of tea.

ALAN: My reason tells me that each day
            But then, what part does reason play
            In love's affairs?

PHILIP: I fear for you.
            I think you might well live to rue
            This passion... I believe it bears...

            Enter ORVILLE.

ORVILLE: According to the man downstairs
            Eileen and Celia are out –
            Some retail therapy no doubt –
            (*To ALAN:*) He told me *you* were here though, sir,
            So up I dashed without demur
            To tell you what I think of you:
            There are few people, in my view,

17

To match you – no, you *have* no peer
(I'm being totally sincere)
I hold you in *immense* esteem
And have been cherishing a scheme
Of giving genius its due
By making friends – *close* friends – with you.
Men of my stamp don't grow on trees,
I'm confident that you will seize
Upon this chance to form a tie… (*Breaks off.*)
I'm not annoying you, am I?
Yes, you…it's you I'm talking to…

*ALAN has apparently been in a deep reverie, and not
heard a word ORVILLE has said to him.*

ALAN: I'm sorry? Me?

ORVILLE: Yes, that's right, *you.*
Orville's the name… Abe Orville… Hi…?
I'd love a chat…

ALAN: I can't think why.

ORVILLE: You're otherwise engaged?

ALAN: Me? No.

ORVILLE: Then can't you spare an hour or so?
Or half an hour? Or *any* time.
You see, the plain fact is that I'm…
Well, practically your biggest fan –
You're an *extraordinary* man –
Your verse, your novel, your reviews –
You have inspired me; you're my *Muse* –
I write myself, you see…

ALAN: (*Under breath.*) Oh, Lord.

ORVILLE: I've long enjoyed, admired, *adored*
Your way with words, your sheer…*élan*…
I'm sorry if I'm wittering on
But I'm…

ALAN: (*Interrupting.*) You've caught me off my guard
And, to be frank, I find it hard

To fathom why you're honouring me
In quite this way.

ORVILLE: You shouldn't be
The tiniest bit surprised that my
Opinion of you is so high,
You've earned it, you if anyone –
Who are your rivals?…

ALAN: Look…

ORVILLE: You've none!
What's more, you don't get half your due –
Yes, people may have heard of you,
But you deserve a great deal more,
I mean, not just respect, but *awe!*
Why aren't you honoured and revered?
You're the cat's whiskers, *and* its beard,
Completely in a class apart!

ALAN: Oh, please…

ORVILLE: I'm speaking from the heart.
To *prove* to you that I'm sincere
Let me embrace you – now – come here!

He grabs ALAN and hugs him.

A heartfelt hug. We're friends now, right?
Let's shake and make it watertight.

He grabs ALAN's hand and shakes it vigorously.

My name is Orville, by the way.

ALAN: You said. One question, if I may:
Exactly what do you intend
By offering to be my friend?
You've praised me to the skies, that's fine,
You've shot a very flattering line –
The trouble is I don't agree
With all this praise you've heaped on me
And I suspect your motives.

ORVILLE: (*Horrified.*) What?!
Look, will you be my friend or not?

19

ALAN: (*In a low voice, to* PHILIP:)
            God, how the fellow does persist!

PHILIP: (*In a low voice back.*)
            He wants you on his Facebook list.

ALAN: (*In a low voice back.*)
            Oh, Christ!

ORVILLE: Are you rejecting me…?

ALAN: That's not the issue. Don't you see? –
            Friendship must have an element
            Of *mystery* to it; when you vent
            This wild affection round the place
            You trivialise and you debase
            A *sacred* thing. What *is* a friend?
            It's somebody who, *in the end,*
            After a prior acquaintanceship,
            You *choose,* not simply meet, and flip!
            Before we form so close a tie
            Don't you agree that you and I
            Should get acquainted? We could be
            So different temperamentally
            That we would rapidly regret
            Our friend…

ORVILLE: How prudent can you get!
            That sage assessment makes me *more*
            Astonished by you than before.
            Let's *give* our friendship time to grow,
            I'm sure, within a month or so,
            We'll be as thick as thieves. Meanwhile
            I wish to make it clear that I'll
            Be there for you, no matter what,
            Whether we're friends at once or not.
            If *contacts* are what you require
            I've heaps of them, to rent or hire –
            TV producers by the score
            Commissioning editors galore…

    Changing the subject.

Now, since you're one of our top men
For literature, the great *doyen*
Of *TLS* and *LRB*,
I wondered, would you honour me –
By listening to a piece of mine? –
Assuming you can spare the time? –
To start us off on the right note? –
It's…erm…a *poem* I just wrote –
I'd like to try a magazine
But I'm reluctant till it's been
Vetted by one who knows his stuff,
So tell me, is it good enough?

He has produced a copy of his poem.

ALAN: What right to judge it have *I* got?
Who am I? T S Eliot?

ORVILLE: Compared to your stuff his stuff stank.

ALAN: I warn you, I'm extremely frank,
Outspoken to a fault, in fact…

ORVILLE: Good! *Excellent!* I don't want tact;
No, you're to give it to me straight,
Shoot from the hip, don't hesitate –
Rubbish it if you think it's bad –
You'd better, or I *will* get mad!

ALAN: All right, if you insist, suits me.

ORVILLE: (*Reads:*)
Sonnet… (*Breaks off.*) That's what it is, you see –
A sonnet… (*Reads:*) Hope…
            (*Breaks off.*) I should tell you:
It's to a woman I once knew,
I never got her into bed
Though once we almost…well, 'nough said.
(*Reads:*) H… (*Breaks off.*) It's quite limited in scope,
A personal…

ALAN: Let's *hear* it!

ORVILLE: (*Reads:*) Hope…

(*Breaks off.*) I'm not quite sure about the style,
I may appear a bit...facile?
The choice of words may sometimes need...

ALAN: Look, for the love of God, just *read!*

ORVILLE: (*About to read.*)...
(*Breaks off.*) It only took an hour to write.

ALAN: I don't care if it took all night,
Just *read* the bloody thing!

ORVILLE: All right. (*And reads:*) *Hope*
Is cruel: it throws you a rope
To hang yourself with, a strange,
Delusory expectation of change.

PHILIP: That's brilliant! It's a bit like rap.

ALAN: (*In a low voice, to PHILIP:*)
Brilliant, my arse! It's total crap!

ORVILLE: (*Continues reading:*) *Yes, hope has scant success*
If what succeeds it is hope-less-ness.
You led me on, which you shouldn't have done –
And by giving me some hope, you have left me with less
than none.

PHILIP: Mmm! Beautifully expressed. Bravo!

ALAN: (*In a low voice, to PHILIP:*)
It's utter tripe, as well you know!

ORVILLE: *If I have to languish in a state of perpetual expectation,*
then...

He stops and takes a deep breath.

I can't face the prospect of waking up again!
Your sympathy, if you have any, will not sway me from
my course,
Nor will I allow myself any longer to be swirled by Hope's
centrifugal force –
No, I'm going to hang myself, or else to slit my wrists
For the pain of hope is gone, when the hoper no longer
exists!

PHILIP: Oh, that was lovely, that last bit.

ALAN: (*In a low voice, to PHILIP:*)
            You lying toad! You hated it!
            'Lovely'! I'll make you eat that word!

PHILIP: (*To ORVILLE:*) It's as good a poem as I've heard
            In quite a while.

ORVILLE: You're flattering me.

PHILIP: (*Protesting.*) No!

ALAN: (*In a low voice to PHILIP:*)
                        Then you've heard none recently!

ORVILLE: (*To ALAN:*) Now, what is *your* considered view?
            Give it me like you promised to –
            Unsweetened.

ALAN: We're on tricky ground –
            Writers, or so I've always found,
            Don't want opinions, they want praise.
            Honesty very seldom pays.
            Last week, a certain person came
            To me – I won't reveal his name –
            He'd brought his poems, which I read,
            And here's the gist of what I said:
            People these days, I said to him,
            Often start writing on a whim
            Which they'd do better, on the whole,
            To try to curb and to control;
            But if they are unable to
            Then what they really *mustn't* do
            Is tout their tra…their work about,
            The awful urge to whip it out
            And show it to the rest of us
            Can prove extremely dangerous,
            One runs the risk of ridicule,
            The public can be very cruel.

ORVILLE: In other words I shouldn't try…

ALAN: I've not been saying that, have I?
            But what I told this *other* man
            Was that sub-standard writing can,

23

And often does, do serious harm –
You could have money, looks and charm
Yet find yourself being ostracised
By reason of some ill-advised
And awful book that you'd brought out
Which sent your standing up the spout.

ORVILLE: It's obvious what you're driving at:
My poem's bad.

ALAN: Did I say that?
Now, to this *other* man I said:
You publish rubbish, and you're dead,
People have been destroyed that way,
Many a man has rued the day
He bought himself an Apple Mac.

ORVILLE: But am I like them? Do I lack...?

ALAN: I don't say that. But in the end –
Or this is what I told my *friend* –
Were you to give up writing verse
Would life for you be any worse?
It's not as if you need the dosh
And no excuse but that will wash
Where writing drivel is concerned.
It makes no difference that you've yearned
For years to see your work in print,
The reading public will not stint
Its disapproval by a jot
Because you happen to have got
Severe authorial diarrhoea!
D'you hold your reputation dear?
Then don't destroy it with a book,
Don't give the broadsheets any hook
On which to hang you out to dry
Not even if you're courted by
A top house with a big advance.

Beat.

They'll trash you, given half a chance,

24

Death by a dozen dreadful crits,
Reviewers are such vicious shits
And third-rate authors are a joke...
That's what I told this other bloke.

ORVILLE: I see. But how does that relate
To my own poem?

ALAN: Listen, mate,
If I'd produced a piece that poor
I'd bin it, bung it in a drawer,
Wipe my arse with it – anything
Is preferable to publishing!
It's somehow both contrived *and* trite,
A formless, pointless, load of...
                              Look,
You can't use phrases like: 'a strange
Often deluded expectation of change.'
Or...how'd that couplet go again?...
Jesus, it's addling my brain
Just trying to think of it! – oh, yes –
Dear God in Heaven what a mess! –
If I have to languish in a state of perpetual expectation,
   then
I can't face the prospect of waking up again –
The rhythm's hopeless for a start –
It's worse than Tracy Emin's art:
To just plonk down some garbled prose
And wind it up and hope it goes,
That isn't poetry, it's crap.
Don't take my words amiss, old chap,
You asked me for an honest view
And that's what I've just given you.
So what do *I* call poetry?
Well, this, from Landor, works for me:

I strove with none; for none was worth my strife;
Nature I loved, and, next to Nature, Art;
I warmed both hands before the fire of life;
It sinks, and I am ready to depart.

If not quite what you'd label 'great' –
Not even, come to that, first-rate –
It's honest, simple and direct,
There is no striving for effect,
It... (*To PHILIP, who is stifling a chuckle:*)
Tittering, are you? Well, you would.

ORVILLE: *I* think my poem's bloody good!

ALAN: You're perfectly entitled to,
But why should I agree with you?

ORVILLE: Well, other people think it's good.

ALAN: Your family and friends? They would.
Alas, I don't.

ORVILLE: I know your kind,
You think you've such a brilliant mind,
In fact, you're just a pompous prat!

ALAN: (*Indicates the poem, which ORVILLE still has in his hand.*)
To find a way of praising that
I'd have to be *extremely* bright.

ORVILLE: Well, Mr 'Literary Light',
I'll do without your accolade.

ALAN: You're going to have to I'm afraid.

ORVILLE: I'd like to see you write one line
As good as anything of mine.

ALAN: I fear I might write quite a lot
But if I did produce such rot
I'd take care not to make it known.

ORVILLE: You take a most aggressive tone,
Such arrogance...

ALAN: Don't come to me
If what you want is flattery.

ORVILLE: Oh, button your conceited lip!

ALAN: Sorry to wreck your ego-trip!

PHILIP: (*Interposing himself between them.*)
Hey, guys, calm down! Let's leave it there.

ORVILLE: I started this whole sad affair.
It's my fault. Thank you, and goodbye! (*Goes.*)

PHILIP: Once more you shot your mouth off. Why?
That makes two feuds your forthright ways
Have dumped you in. He wanted *praise...*

ALAN: (*Manic now.*)
I'll give him praise! (*Thinks.*) I have a plan! –
I'm going to give that *bloody* man
The pasting he's been asking for.
I am hereby declaring war
On men whose writing makes me sick –
One article should do the trick.
Why does one own a magazine,
A literary one, I mean,
If not for just this sort of thing?

PHILIP: Now, wait a sec...

ALAN: Stop lecturing!
I'm off to write it now.

PHILIP: No, wait!
First please just let me quickly state...

ALAN: *Will* you stop going on at me?!

PHILIP: But...

ALAN: Get lost!

PHILIP: But it's...

ALAN: *Leave me be!*

PHILIP: You...

ALAN: Change the record, for Pete's sake!

PHILIP: If I...

ALAN: You're giving me ear-ache!

PHILIP: But what...

ALAN: I won't hear any more.

PHILIP: But...

ALAN: Jesus, you can be a bore!

PHILIP: But it's outra...

ALAN: Right, that's your lot. (*Going.*)

PHILIP: I'm coming with you.

ALAN: No you're not!

Exit ALAN, followed by PHILIP.

End of Act One.

Act Two

Scene as in Act One.

ALAN, CELIA.

ALAN: Can I be really frank with you?
   The way you're acting just won't do.
   Really, it's more than I can take,
   I think it's time to make the break,
   The bad streak in you runs too deep,
   Just thinking of it makes me weep,
   I start to *boil* with bile inside,
   I'm miffed, I'm mad, I'm *mortified!*
   We're going to have to part, for good.
   I'd be lying if I said we could
   Continue for another day.
   I might pretend there was a way
   Without our ever finding one,
   But then, why bother, if there's none?

CELIA: So this is why you walked me home,
   To give me grief? I might have known.

ALAN: To give you grief? Now, that's not fair.
   I'm simply making you aware
   That you're too open in your ways,
   Everyone seems to have a place
   In your affections; you've a stock
   Of male admirers, nay, a flock,
   And it is more than I can bear.

CELIA: But blaming *me* for that's not fair.
   Men like me. How is that my fault?
   They need me, more than meat needs salt!
   It's sweet, the way they all drop by,
   I'm meant to shoo them off, am I?
   To take a stick and drive them out?

ALAN: I don't ask that, but what about…
   I don't know…being a bit less…*free,*

Always available to see
And so flirtatious when you're seen;
You're gorgeous, but that needn't mean
That your admirers get led on,
That you encourage everyone.
Perhaps you'd care to tell me this:
Why is it that the ghastly *Chris*
Is so in favour with you now?
Is the man really such a wow?
Why d'you prefer him to the rest?
Is it his money that's impressed
Or just the general *stuff* he *struts* –
The hundred-quid-a-time haircuts,
The mammoth trust-fund, Mayfair flat,
Bright red Ferrari, all of that?
Perhaps his *ludicrous tattoo*
Has given him this hold on you,
Or that inflection in his voice

Imitating, as he speaks the line, CHRIS's contemporary
upward inflection.

(I'd have his larynx out, for choice)
Or that distinctive laugh of his
Like several schoolgirls in a tizz?

CELIA: Chris, like the rest, you can ignore,
I've told you what I see him for:
He half looks after my affairs,
I've made a mint from mining shares
On various tips he's given me –
What sort of threat to you is he?
For one thing, I suspect he's gay
And I don't like him either way!

ALAN: What difference can a few shares make?
You're stinking rich, for Heaven's sake!
You've trust funds coming out your ears
Someone like me could live for years
On half your annual income!

CELIA: Hey!

ALAN: It's true, though. And you mean to say
To add a few grains to your pile
You'll cultivate a man that vile?

CELIA: That's not a charge of greed I hope?
I'm rich, yes, but there's always scope
For bettering one's situation
With homes to keep up, and inflation.
But please, it's getting awfully late,
Couldn't this little lecture wait?

ALAN: Unfortunately, no, it can't.

CELIA: You bang on like some fierce old aunt!

ALAN: What rubbish! 'Fierce old aunt' indeed!
And if I do, it's what you need!
Now, turning to that puffed-up jerk
Lord Arne, who always seems to lurk,
Like Gollum, in your drawing room:
He's just the sort of person whom
I can't abide, as well you know,
Why must you lionise him so?
Lord Arne! I ask you! What a farce!
His head's been up New Labour's arse
For yonks, he's dolled out loads of dough
Each year to party funds, and so
Receives, at length, his just reward
And's made into a fucking lord!
I thought I'd made my feelings clear:
I don't want *either* of them here.

CELIA: You don't want anybody, dear,
There's no one you're not miffed about,
You seem to think I'm going out
With half of London.

ALAN: And why not?
Half of it gathers on this spot!

CELIA: That's *why* you've nobody to fear:
If just *one* man kept coming here
There might be something going down

But since I'm in to half the town
You needn't doubt I'm yours.

ALAN: Maybe…

He ponders this – then a fresh doubt strikes him.

But what's so special about *me*
That means the rest can be dismissed?

CELIA: Simple: it's you I can't resist.

ALAN: And why should I believe that's true?

CELIA: Because for me to tell it you
Meant swallowing a woman's pride.

ALAN: Hmmm… (*Almost swayed, then:*)
                    No, I'm still not satisfied –
You tell men what they like to hear.

CELIA: I'm glad you think I'm so sincere!
You say the sweetest things! All right,
Since you're determined we should fight,
I take it back: I *don't* want you,
It's finished, off, *kaput*, we're through.
Content now? From today at least
You can't maintain that I increased
Your paranoia – it's all yours!

ALAN: I curse the hour you got your claws
In me! But some day I'll break free –
Christ, what a blessing that'll be!
I try to do it every day –
Suppress my love and get away –
But every time it's love that wins –
I'm being punished for past sins –
That must be it – I mean, why else
Would I endure this worst of Hells?

CELIA: Delightful! What a charming man!

ALAN: I tell you, since the world began
No one has ever loved like me –
My love's as boundless as the sea,
As ardent as a forest fire!

CELIA: The novelty's what *I* admire:
          Bawling one's girlfriend out for hours,
          Giving her grief instead of flowers
          Love as a means to have a row –
          I'd never heard of it till now!

ALAN: I wouldn't need to take this tone
          If *you'd* just make your feelings known,
          No more avoidance and pretence
          And constant sitting on the fence,
          Can't you, just this once, try to be...

          Enter BATES.

CELIA: Yes, Bates?

BATES: Lord Arne's here, miss.

CELIA: (*Wearily.*) Is he?
          Well, send him up.

          Exit BATES.

ALAN: Always at home!
          Why can't we ever talk? *Alone?*
          It's things like this I'm miffed about –
          Make history and pretend you're out.

CELIA: And gain a dangerous enemy?
          This is a man one *has* to see
          And if he got the least idea
          That he's not really welcome here
          He'd never let me live it down.

ALAN: Oh, really? Does he own this town
          That you're obliged to humour him?

CELIA: No, but it's well worth keeping in
          With men like him; one *must* face facts,
          He has some excellent contacts,
          You never know when he might be
          (Though how, I can't as yet foresee)
          A useful asset; I've no doubt
          That were we ever to fall out

33

He'd try to *harm* me in some way –
That's why I'm into him, okay?

ALAN: Oh, you can always justify
Having another *man* drop by.

*Meanwhile, voices are heard, off, of LORD ARNE and
CHRIS in conversation, downstairs at first, then coming
upstairs and approaching. Re-enter BATES.*

CELIA: What now?

BATES: I beg your pardon, miss,
Another man's here.

CELIA: Which one?

BATES: Chris.

CELIA: (*With a hint of weariness.*)
All right, you'd best send *him* up too.

ALAN: I'm out of here! (*Makes to go.*) Be seeing you.

CELIA: Not leaving, are you?

ALAN: Yup.

CELIA: Do stay…

ALAN: No, no, I'll just be in the way.

CELIA: Please…

ALAN: Why?

CELIA: I need you.

ALAN: Those two twits
Are always getting on my tits –
Most probably there'll be a row –
I can't keep calm, I don't know how.

CELIA: Stay…please…

ALAN: (*Thinks it over, then:*) Nope. Sorry. No can do.

CELIA: Oh, suit yourself. To hell with you!

Enter EILEEN and PHILIP.

Lord Arne and Chris are here.

EILEEN: I know.
          Bates said.

CELIA: (*To ALAN:*) Well, if you're going, go!

ALAN: (*Visibly changing his mind.*)
          I'm staying. For their sake and mine
          It's time to lay it on the line:
          You've *got* to make your feelings plain.

CELIA: God give me strength, not this again!

ALAN: I *want* to know your mind.

CELIA: Too bad!

ALAN: You've *got* to make a *choice!*

CELIA: You're mad!

ALAN: ...and pin your colours to the mast.

CELIA: (*To EILEEN, drawing her away from ALAN and to a sofa,
          where they sit.*) Let's wait until the fit has passed.

ALAN: I've had enough! You *must decide!*

          Enter CHRIS, with LORD ARNE behind him.

CHRIS: (*Who now, and from time to time, emits a silly, high-
          pitched laugh, and who speaks with an intermittent
          upward inflection.*) Oh, Jesus Christ, I nearly died!

          *To CELIA, as he kisses her demonstratively on both
          cheeks:*

          Darling, we've just been at a do
          At Richard Branson's place. Guess who
          Was getting mocked and tittered at?
          Clement, of course. He's such a prat,
          Someone should tell him – no, they *should,*
          If only for the man's own good –
          How *ludicrous* his manners are.

CELIA: He's London's messiest man by far,
          An actual, real-life Mr Bean,
          Firstly, his *clothes* are *never* clean,
          You'll see him at some buffet do
          With blobs of dip and bits of stew

35

All down him; you can barely speak
For laughing; then, the following week,
As if he did it to amuse,
You'll find him wearing two odd shoes
With Y-fronts poking through his flies.

ARNE: You don't half meet some *tedious* guys,
I've just been bored to tears by one –
Digby – the way he witters on! –
It was like taking a word-shower! –
He kept me there for one whole hour
Yes, *on my feet,* while he would warm
To themes like council tax reform
And public/private partnerships!

CELIA: Someone should sellotape his lips,
A curse on his loquaciousness!
My God, if ever *more* meant *less!*

EILEEN: (*Aside, to PHILIP:*) They've got off to a cracking start.

PHILIP: (*Aside back:*) Let's see who else they pull apart.

CHRIS: Let's not forget our old friend Tim.
Do tell us what you make of *him.*

CELIA: The mystery man – he'll look through you
As if he'd fifty things to do
Of huge import, when actually
He's off to meet a friend for tea
Or taking his poodle to the vet.
At any party you can bet
He'll come and draw you to one side
As if he'd something to confide
That's so intriguing it can't wait,
Some secret that'll rock the State,
Then, lowering his voice, he'll say:
'Looks like there's more snow on the way.'

ARNE: What about Gerald?

CELIA: What – a – *drag!*
With his perpetual, hollow blague
About the A-list types he 'knows' –

The openings of Damian's shows,
Gwyneth's first nights, that bash for Cher,
Madonna's fortieth – *he* was there,
Bill Gates is 'Bill', and Spielberg's 'Steve',
To listen to him, you'd believe
He knew the Queen, *and* called her Liz!

CHRIS: *Bella's* a bosom chum of his
      Or so I hear.

CELIA: *That* brainless boot?
I'd rather talk to a deaf mute
Than her; her conversation's dead,
Her weekly visits do my head,
I flail about for things to say
While, in her stupid, sterile way,
She kills each topic that I try –
I wheel out the minutiae
Of recent weather – snow, sleet, hail,
Hurricanes, heatwaves, floods – all fail,
Yet there, for hours on end, she'll sit,
Shredding my poor nerves bit by bit –
I yawn, I stretch, I check my watch,
I put away the wine and scotch,
And still she stays, the whole night through,
Stuck to the chair with superglue.

ARNE: What about Adam?

CELIA: Self-esteem
Is *not* his problem, the sole theme
Of all his talk's himself, and how
He ought to be a *knight* by now
But if they *made* the man a knight
He'd view the honour as a slight
And tell you he should be a peer,
Such is his overblown idea
Of his own merits.

CHRIS: *Keith's* done well…

ARNE: He's so rich even *he* can't tell
How much he's worth...

CELIA: What if he is?
The credit for it isn't his:
A three-star Michelin chef's his cook –
Of course he hasn't far to look
For business contacts – his success
Is based on dinners.

EILEEN: (*Chipping in.*)   Nonetheless
He's earned it – that you can't deny.

CELIA: I wasn't doing so, was I?

EILEEN: I mean, his dinners *are* first rate –

CELIA: Among the best I ever ate,
In fact quite possibly *the* best,
But he serves *one* dish I detest
And that's himself – all his cook's art,
Try how it might, could not impart
An ounce of flavour to that man
He's duller than a spinach flan.

PHILIP: His *uncle's* held in high regard –
You can't give *him* a yellow card...

CELIA: Sir Arthur? He's a friend of mine.

PHILIP: You like him then?

CELIA: I like him fine.

PHILIP: The wisest and the best of men...

CELIA: Indeed he is. (*Beat.*) But *there again*
He shouldn't try to be a *wit* –
His natural stiffness doesn't sit
With humour, but he can't see that,
His witticisms all fall flat
Yet still he has to churn them out –
It's part of his omniscient stance –
No cultural item stands a chance:
He'll criticise and carp about
The finest music, books, and art

Since tearing everything apart
Is what a 'witty' man should do,
Leastways, in *his* distorted view.
To laugh at *others'* jokes, or praise
Something they've done, he feels betrays
Naïvety. He condescends
To everyone, even his friends –
We're no match for his powerful brain,
Seldom, if ever, will he deign
To join in conversation – no,
At dinner parties in full flow
You'll see him sat back in his chair,
Arms folded, in overt despair
At the folly of the human race,
A look of pity on his face.

ARNE: That's such a brilliant cameo!

CHRIS: You really ought to write, you know,
(*To the others:*) Move over Julie Burchill, eh?

ALAN: (*Rounding on CHRIS and LORD ARNE:*)
You're priceless! You could spend all day
Maligning people who aren't here
But just let one of them *appear*
And up you'll rush to hug and kiss
And fawn on them, it's 'Darling' this
And 'Sweetie' that. You carry on
Like lovers, all your vitriol gone!

CHRIS: (*Sarcastic.*) Oh, dear! I'm shaking like a leaf!

ARNE: (*Sharply, to ALAN:*)
Why do you have to give *us* grief?
If gossip gets your moral goat
You ought to jump down *Celia's* throat
Not ours.

ALAN: I'll jump down hers *and* yours:
Her malice feeds on *your* applause:
When she demolishes someone
You laugh and clap, which eggs her on.

One could go further, though, and say:
All human vice is in some way
Linked to our friends' indulgence.

PHILIP: Oh?
And why's their gossip shocked you so?
Those were all people *you'd* condemn
Yet here you are defending them!

CELIA: That's his vocation, don't you see? –
To *contradict,* incessantly:
Whatever stance you care to take
He'll carp at it, for carping's sake –
He's Mr Devil's Advocate:
Supposing you were now to state
A preference for some restaurant, say,
That *he'd* praised just the other day –
He'll say it's bad – just to eschew
Liking the same damned thing as you!

LORD ARNE and CHRIS chuckle over this.

ALAN: (*To CELIA:*) You've got the audience on your side
What shots I fire must all fall wide
As usual you've beaten me.

PHILIP: She's got a point though, hasn't she?
Whatever anyone maintains
You're always at enormous pains
To contradict them. It's the aim
Of your existence: praise *and* blame
With equal vigour you refute –
Contrariness just seems to suit
Your mental makeup.

ALAN: Yes! But *why?*
I'm bound to take up arms, aren't I,
When people talk such endless rot
And criticise what they should not
And praise what they should criticise?
At every turn my hackles rise,

           The idiocy is so widespread
           Any sane person *would* see red!

CELIA: But…

ALAN: No. I *will* not leave unchecked
           Your most conspicuous defect –
           Your need to gossip and malign –
           Damn it, you do it all the time!

CHRIS: What defect? She's the apogee
           Of grace and charm.

ARNE: I quite agree –
           The *archetype* of womanhood,
           I wouldn't want her changed; who would?
           If she has faults they're quite obscure.

ALAN: Oh, yes? I wouldn't be so sure.
           I see them all, and I speak out –
           That's actually what love's about:
           Caring for somebody so much
           That any failings in them touch
           A chord within one's very core –
           That's what I go on at her for.
           If I were her I'd boot you out
           Before my last shred of self-doubt
           Was smothered by your flattery
           And you'd completely ruined me!

PHILIP: You'd make a very curious mate.

CELIA: With love like Alan's, who needs hate?!

           They all chuckle at this.

EILEEN: Love isn't like that as a rule –
           No, if you love a person you'll
           Be prone to praise them to the skies
           Since, in your doting, blinkered eyes,
           They will be faultless. Better still,
           The faults they have will often fill
           The place of virtues; it's like spin –
           You turn the bad points outside in –

> A skinny girl as pale as tripe
> Becomes 'the Gwyneth Paltrow type'
> If fat, she has 'a fuller figure'
> Or 'looks quite like Renee Zellweger
> In *Bridget Jones*'; a man with hair
> Here, there, and almost everywhere
> Is euphemised as 'masculine';
> If nervy, we repackage him
> As having 'Woody Allen's charm'
> And so on… Thus we can disarm
> Whatever features we may feel
> Don't quite fit in with some ideal.

ALAN: But…

CELIA: Can we leave the subject there?
It's not, so far as I'm aware,
A matter of enormous weight
Or worthy of intense debate.

ALAN: No, possibly it's not, although…

CELIA: (*To LORD ARNE and CHRIS, who have made some movement.*)
Not leaving, are you…? Please don't go.

LORD ARNE / CHRIS: We weren't!

They were in fact going to pour themselves drinks, which they now do.

ALAN: (*To her:*) You're keen for them to stay?
(*To them:*) Don't mind her, fellers – leave away!
I'm warning you, I'll still be here
No matter *when* you disappear.

ARNE: If I'm a burden
(*With a look at CELIA.*) I shall go,
If not…

CELIA: A burden? You? God, no!

CHRIS: There's Damien's do to drop in at…

ARNE: Here's far more fun.

CHRIS: I'll second that!

42

ALAN: Well, go or stay – in either case,
As I just said, I'll last the pace.

CELIA: (*To ALAN:*) These games of yours are such a bind.

ALAN: What games? They're nothing of the kind.
Quite naturally I'd like to see
Who you most want here: them or me.
Because if we're to…

The phone rings.

CELIA: (*Answering phone.*) Yes, he's here.

She hands the phone to ALAN. She has somehow sensed trouble and is watching him intently..

ALAN: (*On phone.*) Yes…yes… I see… Aha…

The person on the other end of the line says a little more, ALAN listens, grave, then hangs up.

(*Quietly.*) Oh, dear!
(*To himself.*) Perhaps I *was* a tad too rude…

CELIA: What's up?

EILEEN: What's wrong?

ALAN: I'm being pursued.

CELIA: Again?

PHILIP: Orville.

ALAN: Got it in one.

PHILIP: (*Head in hands.*)
Oh, God! What *have* you gone and done?

CELIA: Another wretched lawsuit? Why?

ALAN: (*To PHILIP:*) You going to tell her, or shall I?

CELIA: Do hurry up and fill me in.

PHILIP: This Orville bloke accosted him –
Came up and asked his view about
His poem, which he then read out.

CELIA: And you were scathing?

ALAN: Naturally.

43

PHILIP: They rowed; he couldn't leave it be;
              He wrote an article…

CELIA: Oh, no! –
              (*To ALAN:*) You didn't slag him off?

ALAN: (*A mite sheepish.*) 'Fraid so.
              Now Orville – that's the fellow's name –
              Has had the damned cheek to maintain
              That what I wrote was – wait for it:
              Racist.

PHILIP: Oh, Jesus. What a git!

ALAN: I made no reference to his hue –
              It's not the sort of thing I'd do –
              He's taken umbrage nonetheless.

EILEEN: But this is awful. What a mess!

ALAN: He wants me to apologise
              Or he'll take action.

PHILIP: Damn his eyes!

CELIA: Action?

ALAN: The Press Complaints Commission –
              Unless the requisite contrition
              Is shown by me – in print – this week.

PHILIP: The man's a paranoic freak –
              I read that piece, it hacked and sliced,
              But racist! I mean, Jesus Christ!
              We've got to nip this in the bud –

ALAN: His poem was a crock of crud!

PHILIP: You *have* to take remedial action –
              Publish at once a full retraction.

ALAN: No! Let him file his wretched suit.
              No one can settle this dispute.
              His poem is a pile of crap,
              Foul water from a rusty tap
              When what we need is Hippocrene.
              I'm frank, it's how I've always been…

CELIA: (*Interrupting.*) The situation calls for *tact*...

ALAN: Say what you like, I won't retract.

PHILIP: Pretend you're wrong although you're right.

ALAN: You're asking me to praise that shite?
That ghastly poem? No can do!
No, every word I wrote is true:
It's tosh, detritus, camel dung –
The man who wrote it should be hung.

PHILIP: I dare say. But the racist bit –
That could prove serious.

ALAN: Let it!
I'm not a racist, Jesus no,
But here's a chance to strike a blow
Against a concept I abhor,
That's taking hold now more and more
In modern life.

PHILIP: You mean PC?

ALAN: Yes. It's anathema to me.
These days you only need to be
Black, blind, disabled, God knows what,
And whether you've been wronged or not
Is not the point: to *take* offence –
Construe things in a hostile sence –
Is all that's needed: feel aggrieved
And your complaint's at once believed
And then the whole absurd, obscene
Politically correct machine
As potent as it is immense
Will be deployed in your defence
Demanding an apology –
Well, they're not getting one from me.
It's him, not me, that's in the wrong.

PHILIP: That's not the point. Now come along...

ALAN: (*To CELIA:*) I...

    LORD ARNE and CHRIS are tittering.

(*Turning on them.*) Oh, I'm *funny* now, am I?

(*About to explode.*) Youuuu...

CELIA: Darling, please, you'd better fly.

ALAN: (*To her specifically.*) All right I'm off, but I'll be back
            And I won't cut you any slack!

Blackout.

End of Act Two.

Act Three

LORD ARNE, CHRIS.

CHRIS: *Are* you the cat that got the cream
Or is that simply how you seem?
What's caused this blatant happy mood?
More, is it, than mere attitude?
Has Celia slept with you, or what?

ARNE: When I look squarely at my lot,
I find scant reason to protest:
My family's among the best
In England; I'm extremely rich;
There are a dozen openings which,
Careerwise, I could now pursue
(All of them most prestigious, too)
If I so chose; my sex-life's great –
Every girl I meet can't wait
To get me into bed; I'm witty,
Charming; a dish; I've got this city
Right where I want it. That being so
Want me to go round crying 'Woe!'?

CHRIS: So you've seduced a tramp or two –
Celia'll never go for you,
I'm telling you, you're nowhere near,
Why do you waste your time round here?

ARNE: It's not my style to tolerate
A girl's indifference, or to wait
For months before I get a kiss
As my reward from some pert miss;
No, that's for losers; men like me
Expect results; a girl may be
Exceptional, a real princess,
What of it? I demand no less,

Being a prince myself; i.e.
I *don't* love unrequitedly.

CHRIS: Right. So you think you're doing well?

LORD ARNE nods.

ARNE: No question. I can always tell.

CHRIS: In pole position are you, then?

ARNE: You can say that a-bloody-gain!

CHRIS: You must be blind believing that.

ARNE: Yeeees, that's me, blinder than a bat.

CHRIS: Take it from me, you're quite deluded.

ARNE: You're right. I didn't cut it, you did.

CHRIS: What makes you think that *you've* lucked out?

ARNE: I don't. I've lost. Without a doubt.

CHRIS: You must have grounds, though, of some kind?

ARNE: Uh-uh. It's like you say: I'm blind.

CHRIS: D'you have some proof?

ARNE: Nope. None at all.
Her coldness drives me up the wall.

CHRIS: She's said something. Now, out with it,

ARNE: No, no, she's treating me like shit.

CHRIS: Come on...

ARNE: Rejection's all I get.
I'm spat on, spurned, despised.

CHRIS: I'll bet!
What has she *told* you? Spit it out!

ARNE: Nothing. She's messing me about,
It's you she wants. I quit the field.

CHRIS: Exactly what has she revealed?

ARNE: Nothing. She hates me. Loathes my guts.
It's murder by a thousand cuts,

              I'm so despised and vilified
              My only option's suicide.

CHRIS: Look, *I* think we should make a pact:
              If I can find a concrete fact –
              Or you – a proof that we're the guy,
              The loser, be it you or I,
              Will beat an honourable retreat
              Leaving his rival to complete
              His business here without a fight –
              What do you say to that?

ARNE: All right.

CHRIS: He's off, before he gets the push.

ARNE: Splendid idea.

CHRIS: She's coming! Shoosh!

     Enter CELIA.

CELIA: Still here?

CHRIS: It's love that makes us stay.

     Enter BATES.

CELIA: Oh God, who is it now, Bates?

BATES: Fay.

CELIA: Fay? Christ! What *can* she want with me?

BATES: She's coming up, or soon will be.
              She's downstairs, chatting to Eileen.

     Exit BATES.

CELIA: What can this sudden visit mean?

ARNE: Her prudish morals are renowned.

CELIA: Yes, but meanwhile she sniffs around
              Hoping to ferret out a mate –
              Alas, without success to date.

CHRIS: She's hard on pleasure.

CELIA: Very hard –
              In public, but it's pure façade:
              Because she can't attract a man

She envies those of us who can,
'These idiotic men can't see
My special qualities,' thinks she,
Not being invited to the ball,
In fact being spurned by one and all.
And as her sorrow eats at her
She camouflages, as it were,
Her all-too-obvious solitude
With the *exterior* of a prude.
Her saggy tits, slack arse, fat arms
And general lack of sexual charms
Are played down in her twisted mind
By dubbing pleasures of... *that kind*
Inferior and disgusting. Yet
If men were not so hard to get,
If she could hook just one nice boy
She'd be in ecstasies of joy.
Now, *Alan* is her cup of tea,
The fact that he's quite *sold* on *me*
Is really rattling her cage,
She looks on it as an outrage –
I've pinched her 'rescuer', her 'knight',
So, in her jealousy and spite,
Which, if she bottled up, she'd crack,
She badmouths me behind my back.
She's the biggest bitch I know by far,
A stupid, vain, conceited... Ahh!

(The 'Ahh!' as FAY enters.)

How *sweet* of you to call! Too kind!
You've very much been on my mind.
I...

ARNE: *(Consults watch.)*
　　　Christ, it's late! I have to go.

FAY: I'm... *(Innuendo.)* *interrupting* something...?

CELIA: 　　　　　　　　*(Hastily.)* No!

FAY: I'll call again...

CELIA:	It's quite all right.
CHRIS:	I ought to go as well. Good night.

LORD ARNE and CHRIS go.

FAY: Good. We can do without those two.
Celia, I *had* to speak to you…

CELIA: Let's sit.

FAY: No thanks.
(*Launching straight into a lecture.*) The surest sign
Of friendship, be it yours and mine
Or anyone's, is that we're *there* –
That, when the chips are down, we *care*.
The chips *are* down, and here I am:
People are very quick to damn
And they've damned *you,* dear, as a *slut*.
You'll never make the social cut
If this goes on. The other day
Charles Saatchi gave a small buffet,
Your name came up in conversation
And there was general condemnation
Of your behaviour. All these *men*
You're seen with – endless *hordes* of them –
They drew much comment, I'm afraid,
Censorious remarks were made.
I took your side, of course I did,
'Celia promiscuous? God forbid!'
I hollered. But the truest friend
May find some things they can't defend
No matter how they'd like to, and
I must say, when they forced my hand,
I had no choice but to admit
You…put yourself about a bit.

CELIA: In fairness, as a *quid pro quo*,
Since you've so kindly let me know
The nasty things being said of *me,*
In simple reciprocity,
I'll tell you what's being said of *you*:

51

Last night I dined with people who –
This was at Tammy Beckwith's place –
Anyway, they were on your case:
We were discussing what could be
The meaning, in our century,
Of goodness, *virtue,* if you will;
We batted this about, until
Your name cropped up – your endless shows
Of purity, your 'upright' pose
Were seen as not being truly good,
Not how a decent person should
Or *would* behave – your grave outside –
The way you *act* all mortified
Whenever *sex* is in the frame
Received a lot less praise than blame:
'The woman is a fraud,' they said,
'Because she's got an empty bed
She acts all "moral" and austere
And yet at parties she'll appear
Dressed to the nines and drenched in scent;
Her favourite pastime is to vent
Her righteous wrath on all things lewd,
She'll throw her coat on a male nude,
But all the while she's hungering
For just a glimpse of the real thing.'
Of course, I leapt to your defence,
Said I could not *imagine* whence
They'd gained this false idea of you
But I was just not listened to.

FAY: I see! Well, that's not very nice:
I offer you some sound advice
Out of the goodness of my heart
And you start tearing me apart!
I've riled you.

CELIA: Quite the opposite!
It's to our mutual benefit

To swap our findings, so to speak –
We ought to do it once a week.

FAY: (*Sarcastic.*) Well, dear, I'm sure you'd come out fine,
We'd find it's me they all malign.

CELIA: What *can't* we censure, *or* commend?
Doesn't it really all depend
On age and taste, and not on reason?
Each mode of living has its season:
In youth one should be wild and free,
With middle age comes prudery,
When one's attractions have all gone
It can protect and comfort one
To don the armour of a prude.
Being past your sell-by date, you're skewed
In that direction. I don't say
That *I* won't follow you some day –
God knows, Time plays some nasty tricks,
But not yet, not at twenty-six.

FAY: That's cheap, attacking me on age.
You're *full* of bitterness and rage!

CELIA: What about you? Can you explain
Why, lately, time and time again,
I've heard about some fierce attack
You've launched on me behind my back?
Is it my fault that you're a frump,
An ugly, charmless heffalump
Who hasn't got a hope with guys,
While I just have to flash my eyes
And they come running?

FAY: Hark at you!
Marilyn Monroe Mark II!
Everyone knows how *you* get men
You *sleep* with nine guys out of ten!
You're not as great as you suppose,
I could have lovers, if I chose,
Just make myself an easier lay

And I would soon be well away,
(*Conviction waning.*) If you can do it, so can I...

CELIA: Go on! I'd love to see you try!
Use the obscure ingredient X,
The secret recipe for sex
That you've kept hidden for so long,
Prove simple human eyesight wrong!

FAY: (*Checks watch.*) This topic's going to have to wait –
I should be off, it's very late,
My driver must be on his way.

CELIA: Just as you like. Feel free to stay.
(*As ALAN enters:*) Alan'll keep you company,
He's more congenial than me,
Or *you*, I'm sure, will find him so.

ALAN: (*To CELIA, who is going:*)
What's that? Congenial? Don't go!
I'm really not the slightest bit...

*Was about to say something rude about not having
the slightest interest in talking to FAY, but cuts himself
short.*

I wanted to... We need to...

But she's gone.

Shit!

FAY: I do have much to say to you –
Let's talk then, since she wants us to.
My driver ought to be here soon –
Meanwhile, how very opportune –
I can't conceive a better way
To utilise a car's delay –
We all admire a brilliant man
You must know how in awe I am
Of your huge...talents.

ALAN looks acutely embarrassed.

Why that face?
I'm merely stating what's the case.

Broaching a topic that has clearly been on her mind:

> You know, you should have got that Chair,
> Life can be terribly unfair.

ALAN: Oh, really, I'm no superstar.
       Just what have I achieved thus far
       To make me feel I have a right
       To a professorship?

FAY: Less bright,
       Less interesting men than you
       Have risen further, faster, too;
       Your *stunning* gifts…

ALAN: Oh, please! No more!
       What are you flattering me for?
       Mine isn't such a brilliant mind
       That Oxford's powers-that-be can't find
       A dozen better ones.

FAY: Oh, no?
       You think your standing is so low?
       You're wrong. I'll have you know, I've dined
       In houses of the smartest kind
       Where you've been spoken of with awe.

ALAN: That doesn't mean much any more;
       No, everyone's a genius now,
       Fame is a game, and we allow
       The whole damned world to have a go –
       My greengrocer's been in *Hello*.

FAY: Look, have you thought of politics?
       That's something I could help to fix,
       I've contacts I'd be glad to use –
       Well, that is, if your maverick views
       Do not rule out that avenue.

ALAN: That's just the trouble, though: they do.
       I'd be a flop at Westminster.
       I can't kowtow, I won't defer,
       I'd get too many people's goat,
       I'll never float New Labour's boat,

Show me a box, and I won't fit,
A line, and I'll step out of it,
A fool, and I will call him one;
No matter how my words were spun
I'd have made twenty enemies
Inside a week. Let's drop this, please.

FAY: Just as you like, we'll let it go.
There is another subject, though,
On which I must speak out: this *girl* –

Points off, to indicate that she is talking about CELIA.

It seems she's got you in a whirl –
I cannot say that I *rejoice*
In your, let's face it, *curious* choice.

ALAN: Celia? I thought she was your friend.

FAY: She is, but how can I defend
The torments that she puts you through?
I see how it's affecting you
And I'm, to say the least, dismayed.
(*Planting it:*) What's more, your love is being
    betrayed…

ALAN: Just what a lover wants to hear!

FAY: She isn't worthy of you, dear,
She never was. Her love for you
Is all an act.

ALAN: That may be true,
I can't look into Celia's heart
But it's unkind of you to start
Sowing these doubts in mine.

FAY: (*Devious.*) All right,
I vow to keep my mouth shut tight
And you can keep your *eyes* the same…

ALAN: Now, wait a minute, what's your game?
Have you got proof of this, or what?
If you have, give it me; if not
Stop dropping poisonous hints.

FAY: So be it:
I *do* have proof and you shall see it.
Come home with me, I've got it there.
You'll see she doesn't really care
A fig for you, and I don't mean
These *droves* of men with whom she's seen
But *one, especial, favourite* man.

She stops; she is looking straight into his eyes.

Once I've convinced you, if I can –
If you'll allow me, that's to say –
I'll try and...soothe your pain away.

She goes, followed by ALAN.

End of Act Three.

Act Four

The scene is as for Acts One, Two and Three.

EILEEN, PHILIP.

PHILIP: Sweet Jesus, what a bloody fool!
           The man's as stubborn as a mule!
           We begged him, we were on our knees,
           'Apologise!' we pleaded, *'please!'*
           'Sorry,' he answered, 'but no way
           Will I retract a word. But hey,
           Why is the man in such a stew?
           It was his *verse* I laid into
           Not him! His poem sucked. So what?
           Is that so awful? Surely not?
           I said he lacked poetic style
           Not that he was a paedophile,
           Or'd wrecked his life with drugs and booze
           Or hung about in public loos;
           As for this "racist" trip he's on,
           For Christ's sake, where did *that* come from?
           Only a man with half a brain
           Or someone clinically insane
           Or so politically correct
           His wits were addled could detect
           A single racist phrase or word
           In what I wrote. It's so absurd
           It merits no response, and none
           Will be forthcoming. Are we done?
           Orville's a first-rate guy, I'm sure,
           His *poem,* though, is horse-manure.
           Name something else, and I'll like that –
           His clothes, the décor of his flat,
           The way he walks and talks and thinks
           But not his writing, 'cause it stinks;
           No punishment is harsh enough
           For churning out such third-rate stuff,

I reckon he should swing for it!'
At length he did calm down a bit
And softened his position, thus:
'I'm sorry to create a fuss,
I really, genuinely wish
Your poem wasn't gibberish
So that I could have flattered it.'

EILEEN: At least he's not a hypocrite.

PHILIP: Hm. Anyway, they then shook hands
And parted – which is how it stands.

EILEEN: That he's eccentric I'll concede
But in this day and age we *need*
Sincerity; yes, in his way,
Alan's a hero for today
A champion of what's right and true.

PHILIP: But he's a heterogeneous brew! –
How can he take this lofty stance
Yet simultaneously dance
Attendance on your cousin?

EILEEN: Oh,
That's not so very odd, you know –
Love works in a mysterious way,
Peculiar forces are in play
That outweigh natural sympathies
And chalk will often fall for cheese.

PHILIP: Does *she* love *him*?

EILEEN: I don't quite know;
She *likes* him; she's a puzzle though;
I doubt she knows her *own* mind yet,
She's such a total space-cadet
She'll sometimes think she loves someone
When it's a bit of short-term fun
And sometimes think she doesn't care
When she's in love, just not aware.

PHILIP: She'll tear the poor guy limb from limb.
You know, Eileen, if I were him

I think I'd look for love elsewhere
And, since you evidently care
So deeply for him, opt for *you,*
That's what a rational man would do –
Alan, of course, is barking mad.

EILEEN: I've tried to be the launching pad
For their romance; this isn't rot –
I'd *love* to see them tie the knot –
However, if it did fall through
And he then turned to *me,* in lieu,
I'd take him. Nor would I demur
Because he'd just been dumped by *her.*

PHILIP: You're kind to him... *extremely* kind...
I won't expressly say I mind
(Alan can *tell* you what I've said,
Preached to him almost, on that head)
If he did marry Celia, though,
And dealt your hopes a lethal blow,
Since I can see what he cannot
I'd seize upon you like a shot –
If you'd accept a booby prize.

EILEEN: (*Forcibly struck.*) Philip, I didn't realise...

PHILIP: I hope and pray the time is near
When I can say this loud and clear,
Unqualified by ifs and buts...

She is about to say something when ALAN bursts in.

ALAN: Of all the most unkindest cuts!
Eileen, I have to talk to you...
I've met, and lost, my Waterloo!
I'm worse now than I've ever been!
My life's whole ceiling has caved in!
I feel as though a nuclear bomb
Had just been dropped on me!

EILEEN: Where from?
I mean, who dropped it?

ALAN: Who d'you think?
For ages we've been near the brink
But now...but this... I feel quite weak!
How *could* she?... I can hardly speak!

PHILIP: Just take a deep breath. You'll be fine.

ALAN: To think one person could combine
Such total loveliness and charm
With such a *gift* for doing harm!...
Celia's in love, and not with me.

EILEEN: D'you know that? Categorically?

ALAN: She's been two-timing me all right,
I've got it here in black and white,

Producing a piece of paper which is, in fact, an email print-out.

It's over, finished, null and void!

PHILIP: You're sure you're not being paranoid?

ALAN: (*Turning on him.*) You bloody well stay out of this!

EILEEN: But what *exactly* is amiss?

ALAN: The whole relationship's a joke
And it has just gone up in a smoke.
Such total treachery! Who'd have thought...

EILEEN: Just tell us *why* you're so distraught.

ALAN: (*Waving the email about, ignoring her question.*)
But who d'you think the culprit is?
Only that literary wiz
Orville – the world's worst sonneteer!
And he was bringing up the rear –
Celia had long since ruled him out
I thought.

EILEEN: The man you wrote about?

ALAN: (*Waving the email.*)
This is to *him* from *her.*

PHILIP: Ah, well,...
With emails one can't always tell,

61

They *can* seem dodgy when they're not.

ALAN: Stop sticking *your* spoon in *my* pot!
This isn't your affair, all right?
It's over, finished, come what might!

EILEEN: Calm down. This outrage needn't be...

ALAN: It's your job now to rescue me!
I'm yours forever from today,
Soothe my despair and pain away,
Avenge me on your cousin, who
Has proved so heartless and untrue,
My love has driven me insane
And now she's chucked it down the drain
But *you* can make her feel remorse.

EILEEN: Me! How?

ALAN: By marrying me, of course!
Punish the vile, perfidious bitch
Who's gone and left me in the ditch
By being mine for evermore –
Henceforth it's you that I adore
And with your help I'll pay her back,
The filthy nymphomaniac!
Impromptu though it may appear
My passion for you is sincere;
I'm going to rip that girl apart
By humbly offering you my heart –
If you refuse my plan falls through –

Beat – realises perhaps that he's not putting this in a very chivalrous way.

Which doesn't mean I don't love you...

EILEEN: You're clearly suffering agonies –
Don't take this as a brush-off, please –
But *is* it curtains? I'm not sure –
Revenge may yet prove premature:
When someone special injures us
Inside our heads we may discuss
Plans that we never execute:

Even though giving them the boot
Seems to us logical and right
We end up failing to requite
Whatever wrong they're guilty of;
We sometimes find we're so in love
That projects for revenge are binned,
And rage disperses in the wind.

ALAN: I can't forgive her, not this time,
Not after such a heinous crime,
Nothing will make me drop this scheme
Mad for her though I may have been
Right now I'm the exact reverse,
If I relaxed my rage, or, worse,
Forgave her, I'd cut off my thumbs,
I'd hang my... Oh, Christ! Here she comes!
I feel my fury surge and swell!
God, but I'm going to give her hell!
And once catharsis is complete
I'll lay my whole heart at your feet.

Exeunt EILEEN and PHILIP as CELIA enters.

Breathe deeply! Keep calm! Must be strong!

CELIA: Love? You look terrible! What's wrong?

ALAN: (*Laying straight into her.*)
Name any crime that men commit –
Your treachery more than matches it!
No fiend more fierce and foul and fell
Was ever loosed on us from Hell!

CELIA: You always did know what to say.

ALAN: Don't make a joke of this, okay?!
Your brazenness is hard to beat
But I've got proof now – you're dead meat!
I always knew I wasn't wrong,
My instinct told me all along,
Hence my profound anxieties,
My constant feelings of unease,
You called me a suspicious bore

But I was merely groping for
The truth that I could somehow sense
Despite your genius for pretence.
I'm going to pay you out for this.
What *kills* me is the *artifice* –
If you'd just *said* you *had* someone,
But no, you went and led me on;
And now I'm mad with righteous wrath,
It's boiling up in me like broth,
It's too intense to be allayed
So be incredibly afraid!

CELIA: I'm tired of all these temper fits.
           What's happened? Have you lost your wits?

ALAN: That's right, I have! I went insane
           The day I drank the deadly bane,
           Of love, and was deluded by
           Your beauty, and believed a lie!
           You heartless, trecherous…

CELIA: (*Playful innocence.*) Treacherous! *Moi?*

ALAN: Oh, how *duplicitous* you are!
           But, cutting swiftly to the chase,
           I think *this* ought to prove my case:

    Showing her the email print-out.

    You wrote this email, yes or no?

    Pause.

    You don't speak, so it must be so.

CELIA: So *this* is why your fuse is lit?

ALAN: You ought to blush to look at it!

CELIA: I'm sorry? Blush to look at *what?*

ALAN: My goodness, what a nerve you've got!
           You wrote this email didn't you?

CELIA: Yes. Darling, what's this leading to?

ALAN: What? No remorse? You're showing *none*,
           Though this is *proof* of what you've done!

Waving the the print-out under her nose.

CELIA: Oh, change the record, Alan, *please.*

ALAN: Faced with your own iniquities
You're bent on brazening it out?
You'll claim it's innocent, no doubt –
Addressing *Orville* in this style?
Your fickleness sticks out a mile
But you'll absolve yourself of sin?

CELIA: Orville? Who said it was to him?

ALAN: A friend, an ally in the fray,
I needn't name her. Anyway,
Even if it was *not* to him,
The situations's just as grim,

CELIA: If it was to a *woman,* though,
This latest gripe would vanish, no?

ALAN: Brilliant! You've knocked me off my stride!
A woman! Now I'm satisfied!
No more suspicion! Cracking stuff!
For Heaven's sake, I've had enough
Of these *preposterous, blatant, lies!*
I've *seen* your guilt with my own eyes!

*Rapping the print-out with the back of his hand.
Changing tack:*

Right! Let's pretend, then! Come along,
Prove to me, somehow, that I'm wrong.
This written to a girl, indeed! –
Explain how what I'm going to read
Could be to...why, it's almost porn!

He is about to read from the print-out.

CELIA: This simply isn't to be borne!
How *dare* you take this tone with me?
What gives you the authority,
You *stupid, pompous, posturing PRAT!*

ALAN: Now, now, dear, there's no call for that –
Just show me how this passage here...

CELIA: I shan't! And don't you call me 'dear'!
          Think it's to Orville then, or worse,
          I couldn't give a tinker's curse!

ALAN: Just take a minute to explain
          And I won't mention it again –
          You claim it's to a woman...

CELIA: No!
          It *is* to him, keep thinking so,
          I want you to, he turns me on,
          I've been discovered, he's the one!
          He's charming, rich, the ideal mate,
          He makes me laugh, the sex is great,
          What can I tell you? We're in love,
          Since that's what you're so certain of!
          Now will you *please* get off my case!

ALAN: (*Waving the print-out again.*)
          Just show me how...

CELIA: Oh, shut your face!

ALAN: How hard and heartless can you get!
          Spurned, like an old unwanted pet!
          You have a case to answer, yet
          It's *I* who end up on my knees
          Uttering desperate last-ditch pleas!
          There's just so much a man can take
          But still I can't quite make the break,
          You've such a powerful hold on me,
          You know my weaknesses, you see,
          And play on them to keep me tame –
          A desperate lover is fair game.
          Please prove this isn't to a man
          And I'll do everything I can
          To be convinced.

CELIA: (*Softening.*) You crazy fool!
          Your being this jealous *makes* me cruel!
          Look, if I *had* found someone new
          Why would I not be straight with you

And tell you? Why conceal it? Eh?
How often do I have to say
It's you I love, *exclusively,*
Before you start believing me?
The female sex is still quite shy,
To tell a man straight out (as *I*
Keep telling *you)* that he's the one –
It's…well, it's easier said than done –
Yet still you doubt me. It's not fair!
To tell the truth, it drives me spare
And with good reason; you're not *worth*
The love I've shown, and why on earth
I see you still, God only knows –
I'm off my trolley, I suppose,
I'll dump you soon, though; then you'll be
Entitled to be mad at me!

ALAN: I'm not a fish! I won't be played!
            I *must* know if I've been betrayed!

CELIA: Your love's too selfish for my taste.

ALAN: My love could lay whole countries waste!
            It's huge and powerful and strong,
            So much so that I sometimes long
            For you to be extremely poor,
            Despised, and spurned, and uncared for,
            So that my pure and selfless love
            Could come and lift you high above
            The mire in which you had begun!

CELIA: Being loved by you sounds *loads* of fun!

            The phone rings. CELIA answers it.

            He's here, yes. Hold on. (*To ALAN:*) It's for you.

ALAN: (*Into phone:*)
            Hmm… And there's nothing we can do?…
            Punitive's not the word!… I see…
            Then you can tell him I agree. (*Hangs up.*)
            (*To himself.*) Looks like my goose is cooked.

CELIA: What's wrong?

ALAN: (*In a reverie.*) I'd seen it coming all along.

CELIA: *What* coming?

ALAN: (*Still in a reverie.*) It's the end.

CELIA: What's up?

ALAN: (*Still.*) There's too much wormwood in my cup.

CELIA: Eh?

ALAN: (*Still.*) It was never in much doubt.

CELIA: What *are* you blathering on about?

ALAN: (*Still.*) That's it then.

CELIA: What is? What d'you mean?

ALAN: (*Still.*) I'll have to sell the magazine.
           My life is over, more or less.

CELIA: You haven't lost your case, then?

ALAN: (*Snapping out of it and answering her.*) Yes.
           (*To himself again.*) No justice. Absolutely none.

CELIA: Oh, Alan, you poor love! Which one?
           Not Orville?

ALAN: No, the other.

CELIA: And...?

ALAN: I've got to shell out fifty grand.
           I'm broke. I need to be alone,
           I can't stay here, I'm going home.
           We've so much more to talk about.
           We never seem to sort things out.
           Something keeps knocking us off track.
           But don't you worry, I'll be back!

           End of Act Four.

Act Five

Scene as in Acts One to Four.

ALAN, carrying a suitcase; PHILIP.

ALAN: My mind's made up.

PHILIP: It *is* a blow
But do you really *have* to go?

ALAN: You won't dissuade me, Phil. I find
So much to hate in humankind,
So much that's wicked and perverse
That solitude could not be worse:
I'm going to lead a hermit's life
Free of all trouble, toil and strife.

PHILIP: But must you rea…?

ALAN: My lawsuit lost –
Some sixty K the total cost –
Career in ruins…

PHILIP: Oh now look! –
Granted, in anybody's book
You've been through hell, but even so
Over-reacting in this…

ALAN: No:
You see, that article I wrote…

PHILIP: The one that so got Orville's goat…?

ALAN: *I* didn't print it, as you know.

PHILIP: That's right. *The Guardian* took it. So?

ALAN: They offered me the kind of fee
A wretched freelance hack like me
Can't do without – and now…

PHILIP: Oh, God!
You mean…?

ALAN nods.

                Oh, Alan, you poor sod!

ALAN: The editor just 'had me in' –
           Told me he wished I hadn't been
           So 'careless'; he of course could see
           That quite the last thing I would be,
           Ever, was racist; nonetheless
           These days one couldn't overstress
           The need, in print, for care and tact –
           In other words I've just been sacked.

PHILIP: (*Pointless pedantry.*)
           But you're not staff.

ALAN: (*Impatient.*) Oh all right then!
           They won't be needing me again!

PHILIP: But they're…

ALAN: Important to me yes –
           My bread and butter, more or less.
           See? There's no justice anywhere:
           State your opinions, fair and square,
           And like as not you're made to fry.
           I spoke the truth, why shouldn't I?
           That is my right, a sacred one –
           Compared to what that arsehole's done,
           Touting his wretched verse around,
           I'm on the highest moral ground –
           Yet I'm dispensed with, out of hand.
           Simply because I understand
           What's poetry and what's pure tripe,
           You see how things have run to type? –
           It's I who am obliged to flee
           While he will get the OBE,
           The talentless, benighted fool!
           I'm getting out of this cesspool,
           This mire, this horrible morass
           That *you're* all wallowing in *en masse.*

PHILIP: Self-imposed exile – are you sure?
           This step may yet prove premature.

Everything comes to him who waits.
Bankruptcy...

ALAN: What?!

PHILIP: There *are* worse fates.
Or otherwise you could appeal...

ALAN: No, no, this outcome is ideal:
It demonstrates for all to see
The utter, gross iniquity
Of modern life. I'm sixty grand
The poorer; on the other hand
That's not so high a price to pay
For a full licence to inveigh
Against the mores of the age
And wallow in self-righteous rage!

PHILIP: But...

ALAN: *But* I don't need your concern.
How *you* can help I've yet to learn
So kindly don't stick in your oar
Or start apologising for
The horrors I have been put through.

PHILIP: I won't. I quite agree with you.
The times are vile, in lots of ways,
Decency hardly ever pays,
Depravity's become the norm,
There's an *immense* need for reform,
It's all quite awful. Nonetheless
To go into the wilderness
Is rather an extreme response.
Couldn't you exercise, this once,
A bit of Stoic calm? You see...

ALAN: For pity's sake, stop *lecturing* me!
I've *got* to *leave,* I have no choice –
I simply can't help giving voice
To my opinions, straight and hard,
With no polite, PC façade
And that just isn't on these days,

71

It hurts a man in serious ways.
I have to speak to Celia, though,
Just one more time, before I go,
And see, right now, if she'll agree
To share my banishment with me.

PHILIP: And if she won't…?

ALAN: Who gives a damn?
That means her love was all a sham.

PHILIP: Well, Eileen's in. Let's wait with her.

ALAN: You go and find her. I'd prefer
To sit and brood here quietly
With just my gloom for company.

PHILIP: (*Scrutinising him.*)
You scare me when you take this tack –
I'll fetch Eileen and come straight back.

Exit PHILIP. ALAN is on his own for a moment. He picks up a magazine and starts leafing despondently through it.

Voices are heard approaching. On a sudden impulse, ALAN hides behind a screen in a corner of the room.

Enter CELIA and ORVILLE.

ORVILLE: I've laid my feelings on the line,
If you are willing to be mine
Then now's the time to let me know.
Alan, of course, would have to go,
I cannot *bear* to see him here –
One of us has to disappear.
Now, please, I've no more time to lose:
Who's it to be? You *have* to choose.

CELIA: I don't see why we…

ALAN: (*Stepping out from behind the screen.*)
                     No! He's right!
I'm sick and tired of sitting tight.
You *have* to *choose,* right here, right now,
This dithering I *can't* allow.

ORVILLE: (*To ALAN:*) If she names you then I'll withdraw...

ALAN: (*To ORVILLE:*) And if it's you I'm out the door...

ORVILLE: (*To CELIA:*) Well, Celia? The floor is yours...

ALAN: Don't let our feelings give you pause...

ORVILLE: Say freely what you have to say...

ALAN: Shoot from the hip.

     Silence. CELIA says nothing.

ALAN / ORVILLE: Well, fire away!

ORVILLE: You only have to speak the word...

ALAN: You'll be obeyed as soon as heard...

ORVILLE: You're going to have to tell us who...

ALAN: A simple choice between us two...

     A second pause. They wait expectantly. CELIA still says nothing.

ORVILLE: You mean it isn't cut and dried...?

ALAN: You're telling me you can't decide...?

CELIA: What dreadful bullies you both are!
     Phyoof! You can push a girl too far!
     I'm not in any doubt at all,
     I know on whom my choice would fall,
     Has fallen. But it's not much fun
     To have to tell the other one
     Straight to his face, that he's a bore
     And he can't see me any more,
     With all the pain that must entail,
     I'd rather do it by email,
     Or phone, or just with gentle hints.
     In fact he might have guessed long since

ORVILLE: I don't mind frankness.

ALAN: Mind it? (*To CELIA:*) Christ,
     I'd sooner you now sacrificed
     Compassion, delicacy, tact,
     And found the honesty you've lacked

> Your whole life long, than wore kid gloves,
> Tiptoed politely round our loves,
> Humouring us till kingdom come.
> In fact, be warned: if you keep mum
> I'll take it you've rejected me
> And all of my uncertainty
> Will seem completely justified.

ORVILLE: I second that. (*To CELIA:*) Now, please decide.

Enter EILEEN and PHILIP.

CELIA: (*To EILEEN and PHILIP:*)
> I'm suffering from man fatigue:
> These two arch-foes are now in league
> To persecute me! They *demand*
> To know exactly where I stand;
> That I declare to them straight out
> Which one of them I care about
> And which one's actually a schmuck.
> Isn't it daft?

EILEEN: You're out of luck
> If you need *me* to take your part:
> I'm all for speaking from the heart.

ORVILLE: (*To CELIA:*) I'd say your hand had just been forced.

ALAN: Your stalling tactics aren't endorsed.

ORVILLE: You have to speak, there's no reprieve.

ALAN: Or else say nothing and I'll leave.

ORVILLE: I need a word from you – just one.

ALAN: And I'll be satisfied with none.

Enter LORD ARNE, CHRIS and FAY.

ARNE: Ah, Celia! We thought we might
> Get something straight, if that's all right

CHRIS: (*To ORVILLE and ALAN:*)
> You here as well? That's opportune.

ORVILLE: Oh, really? Why?

ARNE: You'll find out soon.

FAY: (*To CELIA:*) Are you surprised to see me here?
I'm sorry – this was *their* idea –
(*Meaning LORD ARNE and CHRIS.*)
They've told me something, about *you,*
Which I cannot believe is true –
No, I respect you much too much
To think you capable of such...
Treachery's not too strong a word.
I still can't credit what I've heard,
Nay, seen, in fact, in black and white,
And though we're not so friendly, quite,
As once we were, I've tagged along
To watch you prove their charges wrong.

ARNE: (*Producing, and displaying, a print-out of an email.*)
Let's see you wriggle out of this:
You wrote this, didn't you, to Chris?
(A charming missive it is too.)

CHRIS: (*Producing another email.*)
You sent Lord Arne this *billet-doux?*

ARNE: (*To ORVILLE and ALAN:*)
Wait till you hear. They're fascinating.

ORVILLE: Well, come on, then, don't keep us waiting.

ARNE: (*Reads:*) *Chris, you are a strange fellow. The other day you said I'm never so happy as when you're not around. That's nonsense. If you don't come round as soon as you get this and beg my forgiveness I'll have to devise some punishment for you! As for that nitwit Freddie...*

He should be here.

As, for that nitwit Freddie, I can't think why you're jealous of him. Isn't it obvious that I can't stand him? I've lost all respect for him since the day I saw him trying to throw the same screwed-up sweet-wrapper into the wastepaper bin for twenty minutes. Now to his Lordship...

i.e. me...

Now to his Lordship: yes, we were holding hands the other day when you came in…or rather he was holding mine…but he means nothing to me. He's a total non-entity. He dresses nicely, but you don't judge a book by its cover. I don't, anyway. Coming to the man in the green corduroy suit…

(*To ALAN:*) Your turn.

Yes, he's amusing, or he can be. I like his brusque, grumpy manner. But, to be honest with you, there are times – too many times, in fact – when he drives me round the bend. He's an effing pain, and that's the truth. As for our resident 'bard'…

(*To ORVILLE:*) Over to you…

As for our resident 'bard', I can scarcely bear to listen to him. His prose is as bad as his verse, if that's possible. He thinks he's such a great wit, but there's only one funny thing about him, and that's his ridiculous literary pretensions.

In other words, I don't have nearly so much fun as you might think. Please come and see me more often. I love talking to you and I enjoy your company more than you might think…

CHRIS: Or *does* she? (*Reading from the email he is holding:*)

I don't know what makes you imagine I have the slightest affection for Chris. He's nothing but an affected fool. If he thinks I love him he must be suffering from psychotic delusions. And if you can't see how fond I am of you you must be blind. I hope you'll come round as often as you can. I'm bored and depressed and you're one of the few people I can stand to talk to.

> Isn't she sweet? We have a name
> For girls who play this sort of game.
> I've said my piece. I'm off to spread
> The word. Bye, Celia. You're dead. (*Goes.*)

ARNE:　I had a little speech prepared
　　　　But that might make you think I cared.
　　　　There's plenty more fish in the sea
　　　　Even for *this* 'non-entity'. (*Goes.*)

ORVILLE: The messages I've had from you
　　　　　Implied a very different view

76

Of my attractions. Now it's plain
We've all been pawns in some sick game.
Well, why pursue a hopeless cause?
Good riddance to you. (*To ALAN:*)

She's all yours. (*Goes.*)

FAY: Of all the maddening, *monstrous* cheek!
Sorry, I've simply *got* to speak.
You've been a bitch. The other three
Do not remotely interest me
But to treat *Alan* in that way –
It's *scandalous*! I mean to say,
He'd built his hopes on you, he had,
And you do this – it makes me mad!
A man of his...*astounding* stamp...

ALAN: (*Interrupting her.*)
Please, I don't need you in my camp,
I'll handle this in my own way,
A love that one cannot repay
Is merely awkward, I'm afraid,
And were my anchor to be weighed
I'd not be making for your port.

FAY: *Love!* I feel nothing of the sort.
I've never heard of such conceit!
I don't go eating bits of meat
Off other people's filthy plates!
You stick with Celia. You're soul-mates.
Match made in heaven, I should say.
Can't *wait* to hear you name the day! (*Goes.*)

ALAN: I've kept a finger in my leak –.
May I remove it now, and speak?

CELIA: Please do. You have a perfect right.
Pound me. I won't put up a fight.
Unleash your fury. Go AWOL.
Shower me with bile and vitriol
Until I'm wallowing knee-deep –
I won't let out one plaintive peep.

ALAN: Yes, so I shall…and pigs might fly.
You see, no matter how I try,
Our old friend love will hold me back.

Turning to EILEEN and PHILIP:

My sort of lover seems to lack
Even an ounce of self-respect:
Loving this woman here has wrecked
Such sanity as I possessed:
I'm meant to be among the best
And sharpest minds in Britain, yet…
Well, how *moronic* can you get!

Back to CELIA:

For all their justified assaults,
Despite – *because of* – your grave faults,
I love you. Will you now be mine
And join me in my grand design
Of breaking with society?
Come – share my wilderness with me –
That way, you will have made amends –
Otherwise, this is where it ends.

CELIA: Renounce the world? Up sticks and go?
Us in the wilds? I don't think so!
Can you imagine you and me
Living in New-Age harmony
In some…some solar-powered shack
In the Australian outback?
Could anything be quite so dire? –
Cooking our meals on a wood fire,
No running water or TV,
Growing our food organically
And reading by a hurricane light! –
I don't suppose I'd last one night!
I'd *like* to spend my *life* with you –
We could get married – would that do…?

ALAN: No! Sorry. That's the final straw.
God damn it, all I'm asking for
's a love as noble and as fine,
As wholly self-contained, as mine,
And you can't give it. Very well:
We're finished! You can go to Hell!

CELIA goes. ALAN turns to EILEEN.

Eileen, you're generous, sincere –
And beautiful – let's get *that* clear!
You're a great catch for any man
But that's just why my second plan
Won't work – I wouldn't have the nerve –
It's so much less than you deserve –
Another woman's cast-off...why,
You'd surely feel insulted by...

EILEEN: Don't worry. I'm provided for.
I'm not on offer any more.
Your friend here's stepped into the breach.
I'm sticking to him, like a leech!

PHILIP: You're sticking to me?! Then, you mean...
(*To ALAN:*) Pinch me! This *has* to be a dream!

*He sits down on the sofa, leans back, shuts his eyes. He
is in a trance of joy. She joins him there, and puts her
arm round him.*

ALAN: I wish you unimagined bliss.
May nothing ever go amiss
Between you: you deserve to be
Happy for all eternity.
Ruined, abandoned, and alone,
My bolts all shot, my last bird flown,
I'm striking out for fresh terrain
Where I can hopefully regain
A little of my dignity
And where I shall at least be free.

79

ALAN rushes out. They watch the door he's gone out through for a moment, then PHILIP springs up and EILEEN follows suit.

PHILIP: Let's catch him. Working as a team
We might just make him drop this scheme.

They go out after ALAN.

The End.

www.ingramcontent.com/pod-product-compliance
Ingram Content Group UK Ltd.
Pitfield, Milton Keynes, MK11 3LW, UK
UKHW031252020325
455690UK00007B/76